Kaleidoscope of Thought

Rebecca Stephens

BookLeaf Publishing

India | USA | UK

Presentation by *BookLeaf Publishing*

Web: www.bookleafpub.com

E-mail: info@bookleafpub.com

ISBN: 978-93-5744-925-0

First edition 2022

DEDICATION

I dedicate this book to my loving husband, who never once gave up on me and always inspired me to pursue to dream of becoming a published author.

ACKNOWLEDGEMENT

I want to acknowledge my parents who have always supported and guided me through my life. My sisters, who have developed into my dearest of friends always providing me with inspiration. My husband who always believed in me. My children who never gave me a second to hesitate and to all my other friends and family who were always there to provide me with encouragement when needed.

PREFACE

This books holds thoughts, ideas and short stories that brought some value to my life. It holds in its pages intricate details of my life both fictional and figurative.

Family, for Good or Evil

The value of family is too often taken for granted.

When one is young family is considered a burden, a waste of space, an annoyance or a reliance, a life source a provider. Family is a necessity that at a young age is inescapable.

As childhood melts into adolescence a glimmer of understanding may flicker, however, the full weight of comprehension cannot be fathomed. There can be a brief acknowledgement with added maturity that either spark into a flame or smolder into ash.

When all the noise settles and life comes to a brief still. When one takes the time to look back through the rear mirror of remembrance. Setting aside one's own pride, then they may see it, as faintly as one can see a star over the horizon.

Family for good or evil lay the foundation to a
life time of achievement or struggle.

A broken family can lead to a burden or
breakthrough.
A loving family can lead to loss or leisure.

While not the ultimate constructor, family can
either scaffold life's journey as smooth or
smothering.

Family for good or evil lay life's ground work.

Death Must Receive Credit too

One can only live when they accept their death.

Life is of finite nature. It is not eternal regardless how much society and humanity work to extend it. Throughout the centuries man has strived to do one thing: extend life.

However, through the twist and turns of modern science though leaps and bounds one thing has remained constant: death.

One's life can only truly be appreciate if it's death is acknowledged. Instead of being feared death should be celebrated as the event that provides value to one's life.

To fully celebrate and appreciate life death must also receive credit too.

Fear of uncertainty is greater than the Fear of Death

The thing feared greater than death is the uncertainty of what lies behind death. However if that uncertainty is snuffed away so melts the fear.

Certainty in what follows after death is what can give a person excitement and value their life even more.

This balancing dichotomy of life being given value by death but death being feared due to uncertainty,

An anchor, a vestige, a paragon is required for anyone facing the unknown to have their fears silenced.

My anchor lies in a steady sea of knowing that God holds me throughout life and upon death. Although scary and daunting my life will eventually draw to an end and when it does I will be held in the arms of the all mighty God.

5

He is a God that reassures my fears, that allows me to live my life to the full, fulling knowing that when it ends I will be with him in paradise.

I urge anyone afraid of life because of death to stare into the heart of the almighty and find comfort in his grasp.

Whispers

The echo in a darkened room. The call from down the hallway. The words caught on the wind. Whispers are the things that can guide us to our dreams or steer us away from our goals.

In life it is important to distinguish between the whispers that can help and the ones that can hinder.

However, to answer that question one must know what is fueling the voices, the whispers and the calls that one can hear around them every day.

Some voices are fueled by range, or jealously,

Vicariously

Choices define who we are. They make up the many facets of our destiny, personality and soul. Some choices lead us down the paths we have always wanted to travel, while others can distract us further and further from our goal.

I always wanted to aspire to be something, someone of high caliber, a writer. However, lives travels and my own choices took me down a different path. Instead of writing literature and developing novels my fingers tips were must more acquainted to the writing of essays, typing up orders and eventually sustaining a family.

While my dream slipped further towards the darkness I was able to notice a burning light, one that was within my own family. This light is a constant inspiration to me of someone that has strived so hard to aspire to do so much in their own authorship journey.

It is my pleasure that while my own choices have lead me to a more studious and maternal journey, that I can vicariously live through the

many successes of this writer as I offer what
little gems of wisdom that I can.

The Eldest

Responsibility, duty, expectation, commitment, determination....these are words that pave my adolescence and young adult life. As the eldest a tremendous responsibility was offered me: the responsibility to nurture and protect those under my care.

I chose to accept that responsibility, as I strived to fulfill it's countless demands.

At times these demands drew me further away from my goals and desires, however, I would chose the same path again and again if it continued to mean the successes of those in my charge.

Fulfillment in my life isn't necessarily based on my own personal achievement or goal accomplishments. Instead it is by the smiling faces, and thankful exchanges and gratitude given towards me by those I am able to care for, those I am responsible to aid.

I am the eldest, I accept that responsibility. Now and forever.

The Windows you Leave Open

A dimly lit candle illuminated the room. Shadows danced in a kaleidoscope of red, yellow and orange iridescent hues. A darkly shrouded figure remained seated in the corner of the room just beyond the grasp of the candle light.

The figure was death, the candle was life keeping it's shadowy grasp at bay. Never once had death been held as such a captive.

No matter how hard it tried insert itself into the light, to brush back it's illumination the candle continued to flicker. It's dimly gradient beams piecing through the darkness creating an impassible barrier.

The light formed a sphere of that no element of shadow could persuade.

An immovable presence......until a draft swept
through a crack in the widow and engulfed the
flame.

Moral of the story?

Be careful of the windows you leave open in
your life. You never know what drafts can sneak
in when you least expect it, and you may never
be able to anticipate the devastating impact those
drafts can deliver.

Precious Loan

Precious, you smile is precious. Your eyes are precious. Your gentle fingers grasping my hand, precious.

From your waking calls to your deafening cries. From the endless calls to wiping of saddened eyes. You remain precious.

While the word tries to determine value based on gold and silver, status and greed I know I hold the greatest treasure indeed.

Form when you opened your eyes or left out your first cry I knew I was more than happy to let the world pass me by.

To let ambition, attention and acknowledgement fade into the rear. To let people's thoughts, ideas and opinions disappear.

You and only you would be worthy of my mine, my heart, devotion, loyalty and time.

Precious is what I called you when I held you at
my breast, as you breathed deeply your first few
breaths.

Were you going to make it? Would this night
you survive? These cold questions continue to
bring tears to my eyes.

The fear of uncertainty grips my soul and I ache,
as even the consideration of your absence causes
me to quake.

God blessed me with such a precious loan, that I
know eventually I cannot just call my own.

You true home awaits beyond these lands. As I
realize the years you may have I cannot hope to
command.

Instead I call you precious, and hold you so tight
and close, knowing that the Lord God can call
you home, drives me to make the most.

To make the most of the joys, the tear, fears and
pain. As I know that every day passing will
never come again.

I thank God for each one of you precious loans.
And I will always be your mother even after he
calls you home.

One of Five

One of five that is my legacy. A portion in the chapter of the book you gave to me.

It's value and worth beyond anything known. I cannot hope to claim it as my own.

One of five, as trivial as that may seem. Passed through my life like the most wonderful of dream.

Two of five gave me a friend, someone who through thick and thin would be there till the end.

Three of five made us a troop. Whose shenanigans always lead to a hoot.

Four of five saw us nearly complete. With creative talents and ideas that could never be beat.

Five of five saw as as whole. Whose caring heart was more valuable than gold.

One of five, however, is my station. I'll forever
be the first in our quintessence of nation.

Love with a Cost

They say love is looking for loss. That one cannot love without the greatest of cost. While that may be true, sadder is still, one that refuses to love at will.

The choice of love is a choice deserved. For every soul that could ever be heard.

Love can be little love and be loud. Love including many things stands out in a crowd.

A quite whisper to a boisterous call. Love was the most unexpected of the all.

Love didn't seem like an obvious choice, if anything it proved to be the oddest of voice.

Through long conversations and gentle talk, love showed me it wouldn't walk.

Walk out like so many other loves claimed before. Before they decided to walk out the door.

Love can leave one in such a bind. As it fuels fight between desire and mind.

A while this love had the power to destroy me to the core. It chose to be gentle, chose to stand tall.

With a graciously extended hand instead of a grasp, this love showed me it intended to last.

It lased the turbulence of people, opinion and time. As it strived to show me that it wanted to be mine.

No, this love proved to be so much more. Beyond the love I believed I ever had in store.

How sigh in the greatest of relief. As I rejoice in the fact I chose keep. A love that lingered long after any loss, a love that did not come at a high cost.

They say those who look for love only find loss. That one cannot love without delivering the greatest of cost. While to some that may still stand to be true, I chose a love, and I have never regretted choosing you.

My Mother

My mother showed me much growing up. She showed me by never giving up.

She was strong, determined, resilient and beautiful still. She still continues to that long past her will.

I remember waking up early in the mornings and noting her bedside light was on. I remember seeing her deep in her reading, after the night had been long gone.

My mother was proud of her space. She kept it all neat and tidy. She tidied up every mess and made sure everything was in it's place.

In my darkest of hours my mother was there, she held me close, loved me and whispered "do not despair".

Through these memories my mother stands tall. When compared to any other she never drops the ball.

Her contentious conversating and cutting of
words, fueled my dedication to have my voice
heard.

My mother had a way to bear the weight of the
world on her shoulder, while surprising through
it all hardly looking a day older.

Her gentle words, and night filled comforts
continue spur me onward towards the path
wanted.

My mother, as powerful as she may be always
had time for the little daughter at her knee.

A Daughter's Daddy

Daddy's daughter through 5 there may be, he always had a special place just for me. For every girl that called him dad he some how found time to make them glad.

While days blurred into years gone by. My fathers smile never seemed to run dry. It was a fountain of endless joy and jokes. He could laugh at the oddest of hoax.

A Daughter's Daddy he sacrificed so much. He chose a life of dress up and fairies a life that lead him to lose touch.

To lose touch of ambition and water cooler convo's. Instead he knew his Barbie's like the color of the rainbow.

He chose a life of braids and bubble baths when he could have chosen a life of challenge and fast cars. A life of corporate success and leadership ladders. Instead he chose to train little bladders.

His job was filled with pink dresses, skirts and
bows when he could have donned formal and
business like clothes.

Schooling, cooking and cleaning was the like, he
did it throughout both day and night.

A Daughter's daddy is not one to be snuffed.

He chose his little girls, and decided they would
be enough.

The Eye of the Storm

The pitter patter of raindrops pelted against the pane. The rustling of forest leaves echoed throughout the empty halls. The flashes of lightning engulfed the rooms while the thunder caused the rafters to quiver.

No amount of forage could conceal the home. It stood yet quivered under the weight of the storm. It's trusses and beams bending to the force the wind and rain mustered.

The eye of the storm hurdled along. It crossed streams and rivers, fields and valleys. It's fixation centered on one thing and one thing alone: Me.

The pitter patter of raindrops pelted against my skin. The rustling of forest leaves echoed throughout my ears. The flashes of lightning engulfed my vision while the thunder caused my lungs to quiver.

No amount of furniture could conceal me. I stood yet quivered under the weight of his grasp. My limbs and being bent by the force of his hands and fists.

His large body hurdled along. It crossed the disheveled remnants of what once was a tidy room. His fixation centered on one thing and one thing alone: devouring me.

To Be Born Into a Stereotype

To be born into a stereotype is an awful thing.
To have people look at you, think of you,
consider you to be nothing but that: a
stereotyped being.

When every move you make seems to lead to the
wrong door. When every word you say seems to
result in nothing more.

To live in the shadow of gross mistakes and
travesties as a victim of your ancestors history.

When the one thing holding you back holds who
you are, how can manage to surpass such a bar?

Actions and consequences you never affiliated,
now drench your reputation leaving you
debilitated.

It's staggering stereotype forcing itself upon you.
Leaving nothing but misunderstanding
becoming you.

When every glance and every side eye, is filled with contempt and a dry eye. When the pain you feel and the loss you ensure is not acknowledge, understood but ignored.

To be born a into stereotype is an incontrollable thing, but to become a stereotype lies in the decision of the being.

God Give me Strength

God give me the strength to survive each new day.

The day may not be hard, but a day is a day.

God give me the strength to be kind to those I distrust.

Though I distrust I do not have to be a bust.

God give me the strength to be strong willed.

To make good choices and that can endeavor to build.

God give me the strength to yes to the no's

To focus love on the lost and make sure it shows.

God give me the strength to be all I can be.

Because that is all you want of me.

I Don't Need You

Here heart raced through the dead of the night. Each beat echoing in her silenced ear drums. Small panting breaths escaped passed her cracked lips as she endeavored to keep her breathing below a whisper. The darkness crept in all around her like an unwanted companion straddling itself by her side. Her hands were shaking while from her finger tips dripped crimson.

Her back was pressed up against the cold concrete wall as her drenched dangly locks draped over her emerald eyes. They darted back and forth throughout the shadowy room, searching, scouring trying to hold onto any form of dimly light silhouette.

"You came" his voice was cold and damp. His words raspy as the breath slipped passed his lips. "How could I refuse?" she responded coyly. With those words she began scraping her back alongside the blistered wall. Each jotting stone or rubble scraping against her flesh. She grimaced in pain but dug her teeth deep into her bottom lip to avoid letting out a whimper.

"It's inevitable isn't it?" The voice boomed from somewhere in the darkness beyond her. The words weighed heavily upon her soul as the draw was almost beyond anything she could resist. "I don't believe in inevitability. I believe in choices". A gurgled chuckle bounced off the hard concrete walls as it rang through her ears. She cringed as even the sound of his voice caused her to recount endless decades of pain and torture.

"Choices? Your choices have lead you right back to me". He remarked as she could almost envision the skewed smile curling up his left cheek, with his crusty lips parched together.

Here heart raced through the dead of the night, but her resolve remained firm. Each beat echoing in her silenced ear drums, as her mind crafted the words. Small panting breaths escaped passed her cracked lips as she endeavored to keep her breathing below a whisper, gaining her courage to say what she had waiting centuries to utter.

"I don't need you. I never did. And as long as I am alive I will deny you and your family the satisfaction of my soul."

You Are The Watcher

Sometimes I feel the more capable I show myself to be, the more experienced I become, the more efficiently I hone my skills the more I am taken for granted.

I could overcome every obstacle given to me, resolve every dilemma. I could surmount every expectation and abolish all problems given to me. I could foresee eventualities beyond me and recount actuaries yet I would still be overlooked.

 I could build structures, plan orchestras, solve all my families problems. I could establish legacies, determine destinies and I still too, would be taken for granted.

But you....you see it all. You are the watcher, seeing every time I succeed and fall. You've given me these gifts, these talents these resolves, so I will use them in modest humility to be there for all.

Your Final Thoughts

When you lie you head on your pillow in the
dead of the night, what is your final thought?

Do you consider your day spent or day to be?
Do you consider the missed moments or possible
opportunity?

As your eyes try to remain closed and your ears
dull out to sound
What are the thoughts that hold you to the
ground?

When your lay your body on your bed, and head
on the pillow what runs through your mind?

Is it the never ending lists how to and to do's
Is it the never ending mumble of your constant
taboo's

Are you discouraged in your course of REM
sleep
Or are you encouraged as your night draws to it's
peek

As your mind slowly begins to wander and your
thoughts die down, what is the one thing that
hangs around?

Is it the fear that your eyes will remain forever
shut?
Or the excitement that you may finally be out of
this rut?

Are you impoverished by the chances left for
naught?
Or empowered by the achievements of your
thought?

So what thoughts keep you awake in your night?
Are they the type to bring to near or draw you
into fear?

Deepest of Sacrifice

If everyone is super, no one will be.

If everyone is kind, no one will notice.

If everyone loves, no one will truly love.

If everyone cares, no one will care.

If everyone shares, there will be no sharing.

Being super is acknowledged because there are those who are not.

Being kind is valuable because many are not.

Loving other is priceless because many do not.

Caring for others is showing compassion when there are those who do not.

Sharing only exists because there are the haves and the have nots.

While we travel this world as it loops around the sun let us never forget. Value is not forged out of goodness and purity, it is established by the level of depravity and despair that pollutes our world. For you cannot truly have goodness without an evil to compare it to. Right is only right because there are evident wrongs.

Though the scales were not always in such a favor the fall created absolutes of evil for every power of good. Therefore we can always turn to the most essential of absolutes:

The greatest of love could only be shown through the deepest of sacrifice.

Do Not Pass Me By

Do not pass me by.

Though I am broken. Bent beyond repair.
Though I am wounded and in the utmost despair

Do not pass me by.

While I may have fallen into shallow a grave,
while I may be cursed to live among the
depraved.

Do not pass me by.

Even if I cannot muster the power to stand, even
though my will is thwarted by the chains on my
hands

Do not pass me by.

Ignore my mistakes, my pride, my faults. Ignore
my blemishes as my soul inward revolts.

Do not pass me by.

Overlook my travesties, my self afflicted
tragedies. Overlook my meanderings and self
proclaimed inadequacies.

Do not pass me by.

Lend your ever present aid to me in these depths
of despair. Shine me your light so I can be
reminded you are there.

Do not pass me by.

Pull me up from my own disease and decay.
Brush me clean to be able to stand and fight for
another day.

Do not pass me by.

It is only through your strength I can muster the
strength to stand. It is only through your gentle
whisper that I can stretch out my hand.

You do not pass me by.

So I will cling to you my eternal father. Who has
wrapped me in white robes and restored his
daughter.

You do not pass me by. You are ever by my side.

www.ingramcontent.com/pod-product-compliance
Lightning Source LLC
Chambersburg PA
CBHW070611160726
48003CB00005B/2210